Bindi Irwin's

Wild Life

by Emily Klein

Scholastic Inc.

Contents

Introduction

Bindi Irwin's life is an awesome mix of star-studded moments and wildlife adventures. One day, she's jetting off to shoot her own TV show or turning heads on the red carpet. The next day, she's traveling the globe wrangling crocodiles and studying wild animals. Bindi told *People* magazine that when she's home, she falls asleep to "a chorus of birds" and wakes up to "the sounds of the tigers." That's because she lives in the middle of Australia Zoo! Bindi's life is a serious funfest.

But Bindi's life has had its sad moments, too. Her dad, Steve Irwin, the world-famous Crocodile Hunter, died when she was only eight years old. Bindi was crushed. But instead of staying down, she decided to follow in her dad's footsteps and protect wildlife and our planet.

While she was spreading her dad's message, Bindi grew into a major celeb. She has appeared on magazine covers, written books, and starred in movies and TV shows. She even nabbed the Mirrorball trophy on *Dancing with the Stars*! Bindi is the ultimate warrior princess—fierce, fun, and fab.

Chapter 1:
Bindi at the Zoo

Bindi Sue Irwin was born on July 24, 1998. Her parents are Steve and Terri Irwin. Bindi's dad was super excited when she was born. As soon as he saw her, he named her Bindi. The word "bindi" comes from Australian Aboriginals—or native people— and means "young girl." It was also the name of his favorite croc. Bindi's middle name was inspired by her dad's dog and longtime pal, Sui. Bindi's little brother, Robert, was born when she was five years old.

Bindi lives at Australia Zoo in Beerwah, Queensland, Australia. She was two years old before she realized that she wasn't just visiting the zoo every day—it was her home! Bindi loves hanging with the koalas, wombats, and her other animal friends. Her favorite is the echidna. The echidna is a super rare animal. It is covered with spines and is one of only two mammals that lay eggs.

Bindi was homeschooled growing up so she could work and travel with her parents. She gave her first animal demonstration—about snakes!—when she was only a toddler. She told *People*, "Living at the zoo, it's a lot easier to study online because I have all the tools at my fingertips. I can learn from my own surroundings." Bindi works hard. But she has plenty of fun, too.

Over the years, her birthday parties have ballooned into epic events. Bindi told *Good Day Los Angeles*, "I do have fantastic birthdays at the zoo . . . and kids get in free." Bindi's seventeenth birthday had a Hawaiian theme. There were special hula dancers, surfing workshops, a parade, and, of course, cake!

Chapter 2:
First Adventures

Bindi comes from a family that is full of conservationists. Conservationists work to protect all animals and the planet for the future. Bindi has always traveled with her parents on their wildlife adventures for work. She went on her first overseas plane ride when she was only two weeks old!

As a tot, Bindi hunted snakes. She and her dad swam with manatees, dolphins, and sea lions. And she rode camels, horses, and elephants. Some of her fave childhood memories are of "spotlighting" with her dad. He would strap a spotlight to his forehead, and they would go out at night to look for animals.

Bindi's family also rescues and studies crocodiles. When she was little, her dad would

let her help when it was safe. At first, she was allowed to hand her dad tools during the captures. And she could spray the crocs' wounds with antiseptic. When she was a little older, Bindi was allowed to grab the croc's tail during rescues. Finally, her dad let her hold a croc's head! By the time she was eight, Bindi had joined her dad's croc research team. Bindi also got to name the crocs they rescued. She named one Lollipop and another Kate.

Bindi learned lots while trekking across the globe. She can care for wildlife. She knows what's safe to touch and eat in the wild and what's not. And she understands animal behavior. Her dad taught her to treat animals how she would like to be treated.

Chapter 3:
Bindi on TV

Bindi's dad also taught her about filming their adventures for TV. She grew up with cameras filming her. Her first wildlife documentary shoot was when she was only six days old! She often appeared on her dad's show, *The Crocodile Hunter Diaries*. Bindi also got to perform with her fave group, the Wiggles, in *Wiggly Safari*.

At eight years old, Bindi decided to make her own show, *Bindi the Jungle Girl*. In each episode, Bindi would teach kids about different animals and why they are important—all from her tree house. Bindi sang and danced with her crew, the Crocmen, on the show. In one episode, she and her dad traveled to South Africa to talk about lions. While she was filming *Bindi the*

Jungle Girl, Bindi told *The Early Show*, "It's so much fun because I get to work with so many different animals. I get to work with my family."

Bindi also created *Bindi Kid Fitness* videos. She showed kids how to stay in shape, eat healthy, and have fun. Plus, Bindi dished on cool wildlife facts. The Crocmen performed with Bindi in these videos, too.

Bindi had a blast filming all of her projects. She also loved learning from her dad. He showed her that being on TV helps spread her family's message about loving wildlife.

Chapter 4:
Bindi's Loss

When Bindi was eight, her dad died in an accident while working on a TV show. Bindi was shattered. She decided to speak during the memorial service honoring her dad at Australia Zoo. Bindi figured out what she wanted to say. Then she asked her mom to help her type it up. Bindi stood all alone on a huge stage and told the world about her dad.

"My daddy was my hero. He was always there for me when I needed him . . . Daddy had an important job. He was working to change the world so everyone would love wildlife like he did . . . . I don't want Daddy's passion to ever end . . . . Daddy made this zoo so everyone could come and learn to love all the animals . . . Now it's our turn to help Daddy."

Bindi gave her speech in front of five thousand people and three hundred million TV viewers. She told *Sunday Style*, "I was only so little and I was so nervous. I had to have my finger [on the paper] to follow the words because I wanted to read it well." She added, "It was really important in my heart."

Bindi and her mom and brother were really sad after they lost Steve. She told *Sunday Style*, "We started this tradition where we talked about our favorite part of the day . . . It was to focus on something good." She added, "It started as a game but it turned into a life lesson."

Bindi still misses her dad. She told *People*, "That kind of sadness never goes away. It's like losing a piece of your heart that you never get back."

Chapter 5:
On a Mission

After her father died, Bindi decided to work on projects that would spread his conservation message. Bindi told *Dancing with the Stars* viewers, "I can remember being little and feeling that the one thing I want to do is be just like Dad when I grow up. And I still feel like that." Just like her father did, Bindi puts the money she earns toward conservation projects. She told *Sky News* that she gives her earnings to her family's nonprofit organization, Wildlife Warriors.

When Bindi went back to work after her dad died, she shot more episodes of *Bindi the Jungle Girl* and made a TV special called *My Daddy the Crocodile Hunter*. She went on to host *Bindi's Bootcamp* and filmed *Steve Irwin's*

Wildlife Warriors with her mom and brother. Bindi also co-wrote two adventure-packed book series, Bindi's Wildlife Adventures and Bindi Behind the Scenes. She recorded a groovy album, *Trouble in the Jungle*. And she got to strut down the catwalk wearing her own fashion line, Bindi Wear. In a *Today* TV interview in Australia, Bindi described her clothes as colorful with cool messages about conservation.

Bindi also continued to perform in the Crocoseum, the arena at Australia Zoo. She sang and danced with the Crocmen and later with a new group called Bindi and the Jungle Girls. She told *Sunshine Coast Daily*, "Every time I get out on stage I do feel like a rock star. I love it because I'm singing about making a difference and making the world a better place."

Bindi is passionate about kid empowerment. In a video interview for Camemberu.com in Singapore, Bindi's message to other kids was

"Change the world, stand up for what you believe, and never take 'no' for an answer." She added, "You can make a big difference in the world when you believe in yourself." Bindi got to share this message when she starred in two movies, *Return to Nim's Island* and *Free Willy: Escape Pirate's Cove*. In an interview with Jake Hamilton about *Free Willy*, Bindi said, "This movie was so cool because it was all about kid empowerment."

ALL-NEW MOVIE!

When Bindi was fourteen, she was asked to pen an essay for a political e-journal. Bindi was super excited to write about conservation, but the editors changed most of her essay. "I was a little bit angry," she said in a *7 Local News* segment for the *Sunshine Coast*. Bindi did not let the magazine print her essay. In that same interview, she explained, "We're the next generation making a difference. We're the next . . . decision makers. So as a child, I want to stand up for what I believe in and make my voice heard."

Bindi is grateful that her mom has helped her share her dad's message. She told *Sunday Style*, "Mum is the strongest woman I know. She's carried on Dad's legacy and I don't know anyone else who could have done it better than her." She added, "I want to be like her as I grow up."

Chapter 6:
In the Spotlight

While protecting the planet, Bindi has also grabbed the spotlight. She's rocked the covers of *Us Weekly*, *People*, and Australian mags *Woman's Day*, *Women's Weekly*, and *Sunday Style*. Bindi has been a guest on talk shows with David Letterman, Rachael Ray, Ellen DeGeneres, and Oprah.

Organizations such as Earth Hour and Generation Nature have asked Bindi to help promote them as their ambassador. Bindi and her mom were also named Australian tourism ambassadors. The Australian Geographic Society named Bindi 2014's Young Conservationist of the Year. And in 2015, Bindi was selected by *TIME* magazine as one of the year's most influential teens. So cool!

Bindi gets to meet celebs through her film work and at the zoo. She gave Justin Timberlake his Orange Blimp trophy at the Kids' Choice Awards in 2007. She has also snapped pics with Russell Crowe and cutie Zac Efron. Her ultimate fangirl moment was meeting the Dalai Lama, the iconic spiritual leader and head of a popular school of Buddhism, at Australia Zoo in 2007. She told

J-14, "It was the one time in my life that I was left completely speechless after meeting someone." She added, "All that he stands for is extraordinary and I look up to him."

Bindi has also won lots of awards. In 2007, she scored two Nickelodeon Australian Kids' Choice Awards. One was for Biggest Greenie for all her work to save the planet. The other was for Fave Aussie. In 2008, she became the

youngest Emmy winner ever when she nabbed
Outstanding Performer in a Children's Series
for *Bindi the Jungle Girl*. She was nominated for
this category again the following year. In 2008,
Bindi won the Logie Award—an award for
Australian TV shows—for Most Popular New
Female Talent.

Bindi's most recent win was on *Dancing
with the Stars*, alongside her superstar partner,
Derek Hough. Instead of sporting her signature
khakis, Bindi dazzled on the dance floor in
heels and sequins. In an interview with
Entertainment Tonight, Bindi admitted that
she had to learn how to balance in heels for
the show. She actually fell down the first time
she wore them! In that same interview, she also
said, "It's kind of nice to step outside of my
comfort zone and try some sparkles on."

Bindi dedicated several performances
throughout the season to her dad. In a
Dancing with the Stars video interview, Bindi

said, "I wish that he could fully understand how much he's done for me. And that I miss him." Her fave dance of the season was to the song "Every Breath You Take." The heartbreaking contemporary routine in honor of Bindi's dad topped the night's scores. Bindi shimmied through the rest of the season and into first place. When she heard her name called as the season's winner, she yelled, "Thank you for changing my life!"

Chapter 7:
Bindi Gets Glam

B indi's style icon is Grace Kelly, a beautiful 1950s actress who became a real-life princess. Bindi told *E! News*, "I think that it's important to everyone, no matter what age you are, just to feel comfortable in your own skin and rock it and own it."

Recently, Bindi has been trying new looks. She told *Sunday Style*, "Khaki is a part of who I am, but it's fun to get dressed up every now and then." She added, "Being a bit of a girl is always exciting . . . I do like different clothes and playing around with it."

Bindi shares her new fashions in selfies. She serves up stunning looks and empowering messages for her fans and friends on Insta. One post of Bindi in a fab dress says, "When you look in the mirror . . . try reminding yourself about how gorgeous you are and let it shine! Sometimes, it's as simple as buying something new to wear to make you feel good. The main thing is, stay true to you and take the world by storm!"

Bindi told *News Corp Australia*, "The way I choose to dress, I want to influence other people around me." She hopes to inspire and empower other young girls to wear clothes that make them feel confident and beautiful. She explained in the same article, "Just dress like who you are."

Most of the comments on Bindi's Twitter and Instagram posts are positive. Haters do sometimes hurt her feelings, though. She told *News Corp Australia*, "It's human nature that if you get twenty positive comments and one negative one, you're going to focus on the negative." She added, "I try to concentrate on the good things."

Chapter 8:
What's Next?

Bindi leads a superstar life, but she's still like many teens. She told *People*, "My life is certainly not common, but I'd like to consider myself a normal person and a normal teenager." She recently graduated high school and has earned a business degree certificate. Now she's taking tourism classes online and prepping for her driver's test. She told *Sunday Style*, "I'm terrified. I don't know if I'm going to [pass] the first time, but I'll try my best."

When she's not working, Bindi is pretty low-key. She loves to just get Chinese food and rent a movie. She also likes to stay home, drink tea, and read a book. Bindi especially hearts hanging with her fam. She told *Sunday Style*, "I know I can count on my mum and brother to

be there for me through good and bad times."

Looking ahead, Bindi told *Sky News* that she would like to keep traveling with her film projects, but home will always be Australia Zoo. Bindi is also excited to continue her conservation work with her mom and brother. She told *Sunday Style*, "I'm getting ready to buckle down, work full-time, and help out with the management of Australia Zoo."

Bindi's not giving up the spotlight, though. She recently hung with Australian celebs on the red carpet at the Australian Academy of Cinema and Television Arts (AACTA) Awards. She looked gorgeous in a little black dress that was made special just for her. From the red carpet, she told *Daily Mail Australia*, "There [are] a few projects on the horizon . . . I really want to choose projects that [effect] positive change in the world."

Bindi told *Good Day Los Angeles* viewers that she often feels like a teacher. She said, "I'm so glad that I have so many ways of getting my message across to so many people." In a *Toronto Sun* interview she told readers, "There's so much left to do. As I get older, I want to start tackling bigger issues facing the world today." She added, "I want to make as big of a difference as possible." With all she's done so far, Bindi is well on her way!

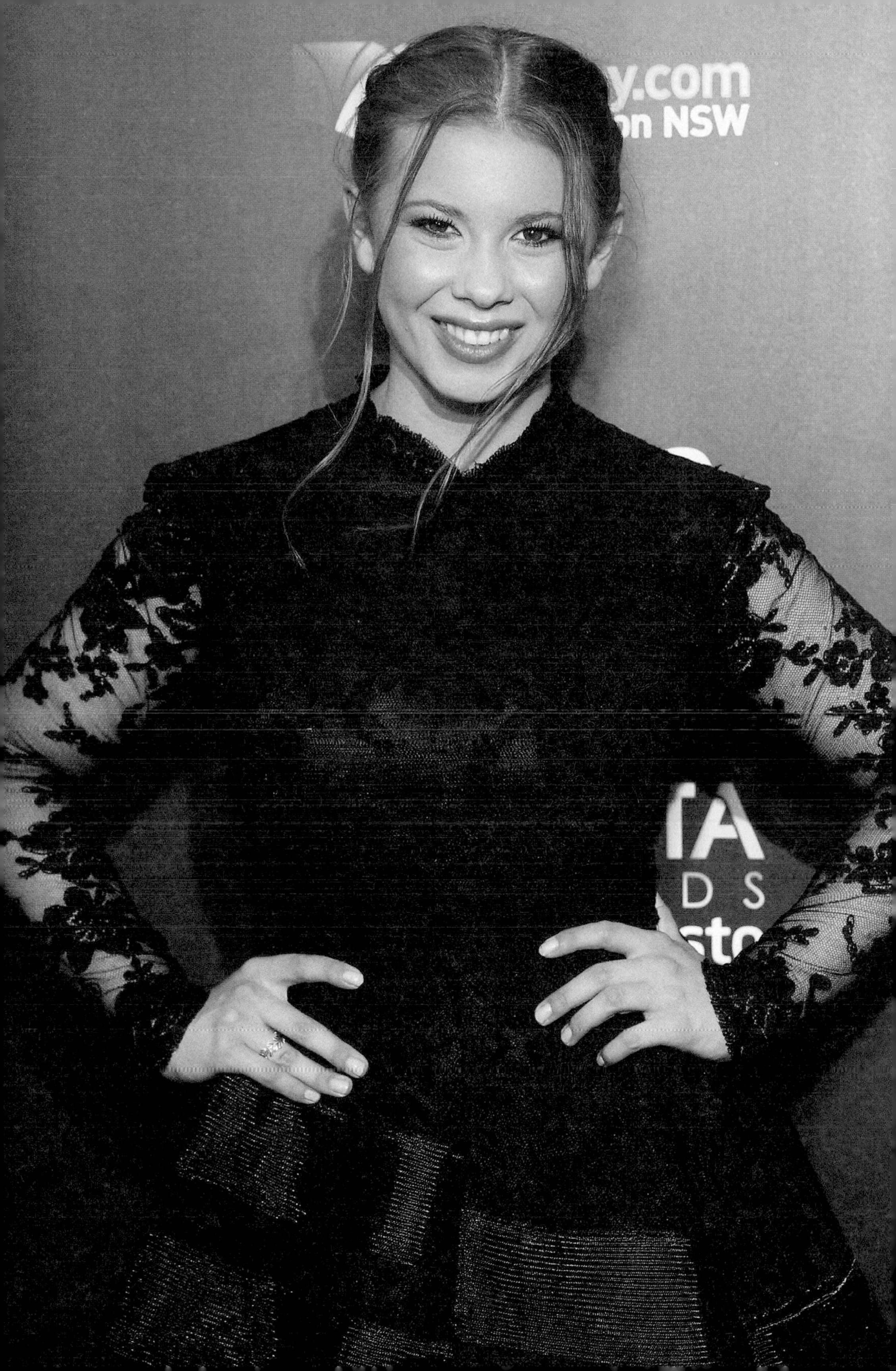
y.com
on NSW
TA
D S
sto

Just the Facts

BIRTHDAY: July 24, 1998

HOME: Australia Zoo in Beerwah, Queensland, Australia

PARENTS' NAMES: Terri and Steve Irwin

SIBLING: Robert

PET: a dog named Diamond

ZODIAC SIGN: Leo

FAVORITE ANIMAL: echidna

FAVORITE ANIMAL HABITAT: Australian Bush

THEME SONG: "Crocodile Rock"

FAVORITE COLOR: blue

FAVORITE CHILDHOOD TOY: a stuffed rat modeled after her pet rat, Candy

CELEB STYLE INSPIRATION: Grace Kelly

FAVORITE KIND OF CLOTHING: dresses

MOST LIKELY WEARING: khakis

FAVORITE FOOD: meat pie and an Australian spread called Vegemite

LEAST FAVORITE FOOD GROUP: dairy

BIGGEST FEAR: bees

BFF: her mom

OFFICIAL TWITTER: @BindiIrwin

OFFICIAL INSTAGRAM: @bindisueirwin